STEPS TO SUCCESS
ONE AHA MOMENT AT A TIME

Stories collected by Denise Ann Galloni

Stories by Jennifer Davis, Racquelle Davis, Sandra Dawe, Jackee Ging, Christina Keener, Joy Klohonatz, Lori Ann Lewicki, Beth Sanchez, Virginia Weida, Jackie Williams, Megan Wollerton

Aurora Corialis Publishing
Pittsburgh, PA

STEPS TO SUCCESS: ONE AHA MOMENT AT A TIME
Copyright © 2025 by Denise Ann Galloni

All rights reserved. No part of this book may be used, reproduced, stored in a retrieval system, or transmitted by any means—electronic, mechanical, photocopy, microfilm, recording, or otherwise—without written permission from the publisher, except in the case of brief quotations embodied in critical articles or reviews. For more information, address: cori@auroracorialispublishing.com.

All external reference links utilized in this book have been validated to the best of our ability and are current as of publication.

The publisher and the author make no guarantees concerning the level of success you may experience by following the advice and strategies contained in this book, and you accept the risk that results will differ for each individual.

Neither the authors nor the publisher assumes any responsibility for errors, omissions, or contrary interpretations of the subject matter herein. Any perceived slight of an individual or organization is purely unintentional.

To ensure privacy and confidentiality, some names or other identifying characteristics of the persons included in this book may have been changed. All the personal examples of the authors' own lives and experiences have not been altered.

Printed in the United States of America
Edited by Val Brkich, Aurora Corialis Publishing
Cover Design by Karen Captline, BetterBe Creative
Paperback ISBN: 978-1-958481-44-8
Ebook ISBN: 978-1-958481-45-5

Praise for Steps to Success

"Leadership has long been defined by traditional masculine norms, but *Steps to Success* offers a refreshing and essential perspective. This anthology brings together the voices and experiences of diverse women leaders, providing invaluable insights into the unique challenges and opportunities they face.

"Through personal narratives, powerful reflections, and practical advice, *Steps to Success* confronts prevailing stereotypes and sheds light on the transformative potential of feminine leadership. Readers will gain a deeper understanding of how women leaders navigate challenges in their lives and create positive change in their organizations and communities.

"Whether you are an aspiring or seasoned leader, this book will inspire, empower, and equip you with the tools and strategies to unlock your full potential and make a meaningful impact as a woman in leadership."

— Maria Simbra
Director and Principal at Ironed Words Productions, Author

———

"With themes of resilience, courage, and self-discovery, this book is a testament to the power of embracing defining moments and using them as stepping stones for personal growth. Whether you're considering a career shift, chasing a dream, or seeking inspiration, these stories will resonate deeply and empower you to take bold steps on your own path to success. A must-read for anyone eager to find motivation and practical wisdom for life's journey."

— Beth Caldwell
Author of *Overcoming Imposter Syndrome*

———

"The reflections in this book reminded me of the power of progress and the importance of learning to turn life's curve balls into gifts. Working hard without a 'why' is a dream killer. The strength of the women authors in finding their calling and living their values is truly inspiring and gives us all the courage to learn, live, and grow into our true selves! The stories are all relatable, in particular, for me, Megan Wollerton's tale of burnout. I found myself nodding in agreement with the words on the page and thinking, 'It would have been nice to know this ten years ago. Thank you for sharing your stories and helping us all live inspired lives of impact.'"

— Mary Richter,
Founder and CEO of Mosaic Soup LLC

"A Book Celebrating Empowered Women Who Overcame Great Challenges on Their Path to Success

"I was honored to receive an advance copy of this incredible book. If you're seeking inspiration to live a more fulfilling life and create something that truly feeds your soul, this book has it all.

"I believe the fastest way to personal growth and success is by learning from the success patterns of others. Within these pages, you'll find powerful stories written by women who have tapped into their dreams and overcome seemingly insurmountable challenges to achieve remarkable personal success.

"I encourage you to give each story your full attention. You'll find yourself inspired, uplifted, and ready to reach new heights in your own life."

— Jordan Adler
Network Marketing Entrepreneur and Bestselling Author of *Beach Money*

"Steps to Success is a collection of very different paths taken by eleven different women and the event(s) that led them to their aha moments, forever changing the course of their lives.

"While each story and career path is different, the key takeaways (for me) had a common theme:

- Trust your gut
- Knowledge is empowering
- Remember why you started
- Stay positive
- Change is uncomfortable but transformative
- Adaptability is key
- Be yourself
- Have a process/formula/plan

"Even if you are not looking to start a new business or reinvent yourself, *right now*, reading the stories of these strong, successful women is inspiring."

— Suzanne George
General Manager of Cushman & Wakefield

"It's so important to learn from others' mistakes and wisdom from perseverance. Whenever women share their hard-earned lessons, it elevates and inspires others, truly a gift that keeps on giving. I applaud all the authors for digging deep and sharing some defining moments on their journey. Well done!"

— Debra Dion Krischke
Founder of Inspired Women Paying it Forward

"Steps to Success captures the essence of transformational moments that shape our lives and careers. This book is profoundly important because it illustrates how paying attention to those pivotal aha moments can unlock pathways we never thought possible. Reading these stories reminds me of my own journey—from grappling with the challenges of starting a law firm to embracing growth as an entrepreneur and leader. Just as I discovered the power of shifting focus to self-improvement, these stories inspire action, courage, and resilience. They underscore that success is not a straight path but a series of intentional steps. This book is a must-read for anyone seeking clarity, purpose, and the courage to take control of their destiny."

— Rocco Cozza
Managing Partner at Cozza Law Group, Entrepreneur, and Business Strategist

———

"*Steps to Success* is a motivational and empowering book that focuses on guiding women through the process of achieving personal and professional success. While there are many books that offer advice, this one specifically targets the unique challenges and opportunities that women face in their journeys told by multiple women's experiences through their inspirational stories. Whether you're starting a new career, interested in advancing your current career, building your own business, or simply looking for a way to expand your network, this book offers valuable insights and encouragement. As a woman working in a male-dominated field, I truly value the genuine honesty this book offers."

— Carissa Perkins
Senior Vice President, Commercial Banker

"This book serves as a beacon of hope for anyone facing adversity, demonstrating that true strength comes not from avoiding hardship but from embracing it, learning from it, and using it as a springboard for future success. It's a powerful testament to the human spirit's ability to endure, adapt, and grow stronger through challenges. Offering both inspiration and practical advice, it provides a relatable story for anyone navigating their own struggles. It shows that, not only are we capable of more than we think, but that the journey through hardship can lead to meaningful growth and achievement. This book also offers a blueprint for turning challenges into opportunities, tapping into creativity for business success, and using personal passion to drive impactful change. A must-read for anyone feeling stuck or uncertain about their future, it proves that every hero has an origin story—and that you, too, can create and shape your own."

— Kristy Knichel
CEO/President of Knichel Logistics

"Reading through the difficulties faced by the individuals in this book makes me think of how resiliency is only the first step on difficult journeys. It can only serve as a starting point. When you have chosen a difficult path, one that you yourself are not sure you can walk, that is when the 'F' words come out: fear, focus, and fortitude. If you want a road map on how to walk a dark path and come out of it better than when you started, read this book for inspiration."

— Terry Doloughty
Leadership Mentor, Trusted Advisor, Human Scale Facilitator with B.O.S.S. Consulting

"As a clinical counselor, life coach, wife, mother, and entrepreneur, I was greatly inspired by the stories written by these courageous and creative women. Although each author and story was unique, I was drawn to the common threads woven throughout the book. Each essay expressed the importance of creating purpose by trusting our intuition and aligning with our values. I was also drawn to the common theme of social connection and responsibility and the emphasis that work ethic and commitment is not simply for one's own success, but rather for the greater impact one can make within their industry and community. Lastly, the continuity of such important concepts such as gratitude, mindset, authenticity and life balance make this book a valuable source of wisdom, guidance, and mentorship for women in all stages of life and career."

— Michelle Fraley, MA, WPCC

Table of Contents

Introduction i
    Denise Ann Galloni i
Emerging from a Chameleon State of Mind 1
    Jennifer Davis 1
From Fear to Faith 7
    Racquelle Davis 7
Grandma's Five Simple Steps to Success 13
    Sandra Dawe 13
You Want Me to What? 19
    Jackee Ging 19
Combat Boots 25
    Christina Keener 25
A Winning Mistake 33
    Joy Klohonatz 33
Surviving to Thriving 39
    Lori Ann Lewicki 39
I Could Never Do That… or Can I? 45
    Beth Sanchez 45
Flip the Script to Win More Referrals 51
    Virginia Weida 51
Never a Failure. Always a Lesson. 61
    Jackie Williams 61
Rig to Renewal: Turning Burnout into a Wellness Mission 71

Megan Wollerton 71
About the Alzheimer's Association 77

Introduction

Denise Ann Galloni

Have you ever been in the middle of a situation and wondered how it might impact your life? Maybe you didn't realize it at first, but later, when you looked back, the aha moment clicked for you. This is how I am. I need to process things before I realize the impact of the event.

We all have these moments, whether you call them aha moments, gut feelings, or life-changing events. Successful people pay attention and learn from these moments. They use these moments to shape their lives in ways they never thought possible.

This anthology will introduce you to eleven successful women, each of whom has a unique story that involves changes in their lives, whether it is a career change, leaving their stable jobs to strike out and fulfill their dreams, or other events that impacted the trajectory of their lives.

Maybe starting your own business, working at Disney, or joining the army is not on your radar. That's okay. That's not what this book is about. These wonderful stories emphasize how these eleven women recognized that something was missing, and when that aha moment came, they grabbed it and worked for the opportunity to make a change. Their stories are powerful and empowering.

Knowing when and how to act in these moments is all part of the puzzle. Is it scary? Heck yeah, it is. Is there always a safety net to catch you if you fall? Nope. Can these types of moments change your life in ways you never knew? Absolutely!

You will understand the title *Steps to Success: One Aha Moment at a Time* after you read these stories. Some will resonate with you and cause you to look at your life and ponder what aha moments occurred that you can capitalize on either now or later.

The key is to use these aha moments in your life to walk in your own steps and begin to chart your own unique path to success.

Why am I so passionate about these aha moments? One of these moments happened to me, and it wasn't until years later that I realized how it morphed me into the person I am today.

My first college class *ever* was accounting. I was working full-time and went to a community college at night. Why I would start out with accounting is one of the great mysteries of the world. I wasn't a big fan of math, but I thought it was a great course to begin with and get my feet wet in the college experience. If I hadn't taken that course, my aha moment would never have happened. Would the trajectory of my life and career be the same as it is today? There is no way to predict. But back to my tale of woe and my aha moment…

As you can imagine from how I set up this story, I struggled with accounting. In fact, I was terrible. As I mentioned, I was also working a full-time job (having nothing to do with accounting), and one night a week, I'd drive to the community college to take this course. Sunday was my time to do my homework and try to learn the concepts for the next week.

Let me paint the picture of my Sunday. I would always wake up with dread that I had to work on accounting. I hated it so much, and I didn't understand anything the professor said in class or asked for in the assignments. I would spend countless hours at the dining room table listening to my mother tell me it would be alright. Meanwhile, I'd try to make the numbers on my balance sheet work as they were supposed to on my tear-stained paper. Adding to the difficulty was the fact I could not read said numbers because I erased them so many times, and the paper was ripped everywhere. I would pack up the assignment, knowing it was wrong and wishing I had a dog to eat my homework. Then I'd just wait until class.

Introduction

In class, we would go over the homework, and I would softly cry in my seat pondering many questions. *Why did everyone but me understand this language of numbers? Why did I take accounting when I was not smart enough to do this course?* (At this point I had no self-confidence at all.) *How can I at least earn a C grade so my employer will reimburse me?*

After a few weeks, the professor took pity on me. He told me to call him at home on Sunday, and he would try to walk me through the assignments. After two weeks of him explaining them to me, I would eventually catch on and it would click like a light switch (his words, not mine). I started figuring out how to make those damned numbers work. I was actually learning accounting! In time, the torn, tear-stained pages became fewer, and I didn't dread waking up on Sunday morning. This was the best professor I ever had throughout my entire bachelor's and master's degree experience.

In class, I was so intent on listening to every word he said. He was a miracle worker, after all. One time while chatting with us, he said something out of the ordinary. It was a simple story of when he was in the service. It has been so long; I don't remember which branch. The sergeant (or whoever his superior was) kept offering the platoon different classes to take to keep them busy and expand their horizons. My professor wasn't interested, however, and kept ignoring the classes.

Finally, he was called into the office to speak with his superior. I remember exactly what he said his superior said to him. "Son," he said, "you have not been taking advantage of any of these fun classes because you do not feel they are important to your military career. Let me tell you something: knowledge is power, no matter what happens in your life. No one can ever take that knowledge and power away from you. If there is a knitting class, take it. You may not want to learn how to knit, but you never know when a time will come when you can use that knowledge or something you learned in that class."

The class laughed as did the professor picturing a soldier in uniform with his weapon on the table and a knitting needle and yarn on his lap.

I didn't think of that story again until certain opportunities came to me in my life, and I realized I needed to learn from them. For example, my family laughs at my eclectic taste in books. I have always been an avid reader, and over time, I've expanded my selection to all different kinds of topics. I get strange looks when I am not watching the latest thriller or the latest Netflix show because I would rather be reading. Looking for a documentary to watch one day, I said to myself, *Sure, I'll check out the honey badger...quite an interesting animal.*

Eventually, I became a well-rounded professional who could hold my own in a conversation and was able to use some of the trivia I'd picked up. I began my business in 2014 and had no idea what to do. I would attend networking events and listen intently to anyone giving a presentation. *Okay,* I'd think to myself, *you're a funeral director or you own a printing company. I get it. You are successful. What can I do in my business to become more successful using what these others have learned?* I have read Napoleon Hill's *Think and Grow Rich* too many times to count, and I love to discuss it with anyone at any time. It had such an impact on me.

Sitting in that accounting class was my aha moment, though I didn't realize it until years later. I have lived by the mantra that knowledge is power, and no one can ever take it from me. No one and no situation can take that power away from you—not a divorce, not the loss of a job, not a change in career—it is all knowledge that has helped you become the professional you are today.

I hope you enjoy the stories from these eleven, incredible, successful women. Look for your own aha moments where you least expect them. They happen for a reason. Treasure them, nurture them, and use them for your path to walk your steps to success.

Introduction

Oh! I almost forgot to tell you what happened in that very first accounting class...

I received a B- grade and was so happy. By the end of the class, it did in fact all click, and I earned 100 percent on the final. It clicked so much that I took three other accounting classes and aced them all with an A or A+. I was ready to change my career to accounting until I realized I needed to take "tax accounting." But I didn't think I wanted to go that route. So that was the end of my accounting aspirations. In the end, I did okay without becoming a CPA.

I still wonder what made me take that accounting class. Maybe it was supposed to happen, me being in that classroom, hearing that story about learning everything you can. Today I consider myself a constant learner.

Take time to appreciate all that is around you and be cognizant of those aha moments. They may sneak up on you without you realizing it. I have had several through the years, but none as impactful as my experiences with that accounting professor.

I wish you a lifetime of aha moments, a lifetime of learning, and a lifetime of expanding your knowledge and increasing your empowerment. You got this.

Keep walking the steps to success!

Denise Ann

Denise Ann Galloni
Author, Speaker, TV Host
DeniseAnnGalloni.com

About Denise

Ever since being named "The Quietest Girl" in her senior class, Denise Ann Galloni has focused on using her voice and helping others find theirs. Working with organizations and individuals through her company, DG Training Solutions, Inc., Denise has delivered over five hundred presentations and keynotes to countless professionals who want to be better communicators and better leaders.

Denise's passion for leadership, communication, and corporate training has earned her a multitude of awards and recognitions, including being named a two-time distinguished Toastmaster and receiving the Business Choice Award for Corporate Training at the Pittsburgh Business Show.

Introduction

She is the host of the award-winning TV show *Empowering You*, has been a featured guest on several domestic and international podcasts, and has been featured in more than one hundred media outlets. Her newest show is called *Helping Hands* and features local community programs and people helping people.

Denise is the author of *Find Your VOICE: 5 Keys to Lead and Empower Others*. She is also a contributor to *Unleashing Your Soul Level Magic*, a book that achieved Amazon bestseller status in one day. She and James Malinchak, the most requested, in-demand business and motivational keynote speaker and marketing consultant in the world, are co-writing a new book called *Success is a Choice: Inspiring Thoughts to Jumpstart Your Success*, due to be released in 2025.

Denise received her master of science in professional leadership from Carlow University in Pittsburgh, Pa. She regularly speaks for a variety of audiences (ranging from entry-level to experienced executives) including corporations, business groups, associations, and other organizations.

When she is not hosting her TV shows, reading the new professional development book, or spending time with her family, you can find Denise speaking in-person and virtually to groups of twenty to more than twenty thousand.

Any organization looking for an engaging speaker, who will educate, motivate, and empower their audience to be better communicators and better leaders, should book Denise for keynote and/or workshop training. Find out more details at DeniseAnnGalloni.com, and follow her on Facebook and LinkedIn (search "Denise Ann Galloni") for information on her workshops and powerful ideas to help you succeed in your own business, contact her at info@deniseanngalloni.com.

Emerging from a Chameleon State of Mind

Jennifer Davis

Have you ever felt like you are shifting, maybe changing your colors? I found myself being a chameleon of sorts for many years. This all started when I moved in my youth and had to make friends all over again. Moving into a new situation and trying to fit in as a teenager or an adult can be so difficult.

My first move was from Ohio to Texas between the fifth and sixth grades. I moved from elementary school to junior high. The students I encountered were mean and hateful with their words. They made me feel like I didn't belong. The one phrase I heard the most was "Yankee, go home." Really? Like I had a choice to be there. If it had been up to me, I would have gone back to Ohio. But since it couldn't, I just changed schools and adopted a Texas accent to fit in.

Little did I know, another move was coming between my sophomore and junior years of high school. This move saw me go from Texas to Arizona. Here I was moving again to a new place. Again, I needed to try to fit in. On my first day of school, I dressed in something I would typically wear to school in Texas including dress pants, a blouse, and short ankle boots. I was extremely out of place. Plus, I sounded different due to my Texas accent. The good news was the students were kinder, as much as kids are in high school. I still had to restart again, learn a new school, make friends, and adjust to a new area.

These two moves were traumatic and life-changing. I learned to be a chameleon in order to feel like I fit in and to find acceptance. This allowed me to show a part of myself but not my whole self. I functioned in this state for many years as an adult.

My ability to be a chameleon served me well as I attended in-state college, changed jobs, and made future moves. I moved from Arizona to Colorado for a promotion with the phone company. The change also resulted in me needing a new wardrobe to survive in the cold and snow. The deal I made myself was to stay in Colorado for at least one year. After that, if I was still missing living in Arizona, I would give myself permission to consider moving back.

The time I spent in Colorado was when I started putting away the chameleon persona more often. The job I moved there for only lasted a few years. Our call center was eventually outsourced, and I decided the company no longer served me. Plus, I had met my husband and was going to be married a few months after leaving the phone company. So, I moved on to retail for a short while and then to the local blood center.

I found my niche at the blood center, though there was so much to learn. I had to adapt to new terminology and took on different positions at the company. I also received my MBA while working full-time. Why does this matter? Because I found I was good at certain things.

First, the knowledge I gained at the phone company helped me transform the call center at the blood center. I was challenged by the team I was working with. They had never utilized metrics before; the team just made calls at the pace they wanted. I was accused of fixing things with the phones so the team would fail. Many days I went home frustrated and doubting myself. Once again, it would have been easy to hide behind the chameleon. Instead, I chose to move forward as me—all of me.

I moved into two other positions within the blood center. A month after I started my MBA program, I was offered the open account manager position. I would have my own territory and would learn a different part of our business by recruiting donors in person rather than leading a team to do it over the phone. One year after starting the position, my manager was leaving and her position as a manager in business development opened up. I decided to apply. After a tough round of interviews, I was told they hired someone else; however, I did have a good interview. Deflated, I started to question my next move. Plus, I felt the tug of the chameleon again. I wanted to hide my feelings and put on the brave face of not getting a position that I felt I would excel at. Luckily, a month later, the person they hired never started, and I was offered the job. I kept the chameleon act up for a bit while adjusting to the position and finishing my MBA. I ended up serving in the business development manager position for over ten years. It felt like the chameleon was gone for good, and I had finally found my stride.

Seven years ago I moved to PA, and the chameleon once again was ready to protect me. I was in a new place and received a promotion with the blood center. I soon found that even though it was the same industry, things were done differently.

I started to wonder what I got myself into and where exactly I was living. Plus, I had so many years without feeling like a chameleon, and I wasn't sure I wanted to wear that persona again. I knew that it dimmed my light and never brought me happiness. The chameleon made me feel fake and not completely fulfilled.

So I worked hard and changed my mindset. Today I am living in a new place, and it is different than all the other places I have lived. There are things I have to offer to people when I meet them. Plus, by being my true self, my authentic self, I can learn from and appreciate others around me. I am finding I do not need the chameleon to be my persona. While this served me well in my youth and when my career was just starting out, I realize that I no longer need the chameleon as my daily partner.

I do wonder, at times, what I have missed by leaning on my chameleon defense persona. I wonder what opportunities and experiences I've missed. That said, I remind myself I cannot go back in time. I need to look forward. I find that by hanging up the chameleon, I'm having new experiences and pushing boundaries. Growth happens when you're outside of your comfort zone. The chameleon is my comfort zone, and I look forward to ongoing growth in my life.

This is not to say the chameleon was a bad persona to have at times or that I regret it. It was a defense mechanism. It got me through some tough times and difficult situations. But you can't always live in the chameleon persona. Your true light does not come through when meeting with others or when experiencing a situation. Anyone you meet will not get to see or experience the real you.

Each of us is a unique individual. Each of us brings something unique to the table, the conversation, or the experience. The world is a better place when we allow our true light to shine on others. Our personality should never be dimmed because of a tough situation or out of fear. The next person you meet could be positively impacted by you and what you represent. Likewise, the next person you meet could rock your world and give you exactly what you need at that time.

Take time today to make sure you are allowing yourself to show who you are. You could be the light someone is looking for. Just think of the collective difference we can make together by being authentic and genuine! I see this as the ultimate pay-it-forward.

If you find you have a chameleon persona, consider placing it in the back of your closet. I would not recommend you completely discard it, though, as there could be a time when you will need it as a protective measure. My chameleon is now on sabbatical for an unspecified time. I know if I need it, I can pull it out. Most importantly, I need to make sure the chameleon doesn't become an unwanted guest in the future.

Join me, and let your light shine for everyone to see. What you have to say is important, and others benefit from you being in their life. Never dim your light for others or for yourself!

About Jennifer

Jennifer Davis is a senior director of blood donor recruitment at Vitalant for the northeast division. She has served in multiple roles over her almost twenty-three-year career in blood banking. All of her positions have included asking people to take time and make a blood donation. Jennifer has been a member of Polka Dot Powerhouse, a women's connection company, for seven years and the managing director of the Pittsburgh chapter since September of 2021. She finds inspiration in connecting and celebrating with women. She believes that women do not celebrate ourselves enough, always putting others ahead and being their cheerleader.

Jennifer has been married to her husband, Dale, for twenty-four years. They moved from the Denver, Colo., area to

Steps to Success

Pittsburgh, Pa., in September of 2017. While they do miss the Rocky Mountains and the more than three hundred days of sun in Denver from time to time, they love how much the Pittsburgh area has for them to explore and agree that the eastern part of the United States is beautiful, too. They especially love just getting in the car for an "adventure" day. This could mean going to a restaurant, finding some fun shops, or seeing a different part of the area.

From Fear to Faith

Racquelle Davis

I'm a small-town girl who didn't grow up with much but a loving family and a willingness to learn anything I could. Raised by a hard-working single mother, I've not had the easiest start to life, but I'm grateful for the beautiful people in my life along the way.

All my life I've had this feeling that has kept me going, striving, and pushing forward to tackle the next thing in my life. This drive, as I call it, has been extremely helpful; however, I was unaware of it until I hit burnout and wanted to learn how to slow down. At that time, I found it was quite a challenge to turn off the anxiety and the constant hustling and just sit and allow life to happen.

I hit the ground running when I was young. You see, I graduated high school at the age of seventeen. I was an honors student, earning college credit for high school classes while also holding down two part-time jobs. I went to Clarion University of Pennsylvania, and in just two and a half years, I graduated with a bachelor's degree in business administration at age twenty, in December 2008. This was a challenging time to enter the job market as this was in the midst of the Great Recession.

With high hopes and an optimistic outlook, I applied for jobs in the Pittsburgh area. As fate would have it, I landed a job in logistics and discovered I liked to learn. So I decided to give it a shot! Little did I know that I would fall in *love* with the fast-paced problem-solving and negotiation life of a freight broker. I worked for that same company for eight years, moving up the corporate ladder every two and a half years. Soon I felt an internal itch that urged me to move on. Eventually, I changed companies and spent a few years there until I again got the urge to change things in my life. This itch or urge is something internal that cannot be ignored.

Over the years of my adult life, I've learned to tune in and listen to this internal driving force or, as I sometimes called it, my "gut feeling." Each time I felt bored in a position or ready to earn more money, I started to feel unsettled in my career, life, and body. Looking back, this is a pattern that I now recognize, but at the time, I didn't even know it was happening.

In April of 2019, the biggest shift in my life thus far happened. I was burnt out, overwhelmed, and searching for answers. In a yoga meditation one night, I had an epiphany. I was told to quit my job, and that it would all work out. The next day, that's just what I did! It was so unlike me to let go of such a secure safety net as my career without a backup plan or next step. But I knew deep down—I *knew*—I had to do it. The challenge was not allowing the fear to hold me back in crippling anxiety but to lean into my faith in knowing I was being divinely guided to this moment of time; to lean on my faith that this is a friendly universe and everything is always unfolding exactly as it's meant to be; to lean on my faith that I had it inside of me to accomplish all of my dreams.

Fast forward through the years of COVID to the moment I am writing this chapter, the end of 2024, and I am again being led to lean into my faith, let go of what I used to know to be true, and *trust* that I am exactly where I'm supposed to be in this lifetime. My company, Zen Freight Solutions Inc., has now reached five years in business, with year over year of steady growth, and I have finally begun to slow down personally. The process of slowing down is directly connected to the faith I have.

So maybe you are currently in this situation. You know that where you are right now doesn't *feel* like your best and most authentic life, but you also have *no idea* of any possibility of changing it.

This place can be overwhelmingly scary!

It is also an extremely defining point in your life. I'm here to tell you that while in that place of hell, you may walk, run, crawl, or drag yourself through, but whatever you do, do *not* stay there! This place (of time, physical situation, or scenario) can feel like you are in a dark tunnel. You can see your current life behind you. Maybe you're even running *away* from it? Meanwhile, in front of you is pitch-black nothingness. It's so dark that you can't see your hand in front of your face. As your sight is diminished, all other body senses activate. Your breathing increases, your heart pounds and feels like it's in your throat, your ears are on high alert for any possible danger that may be ahead, and your entire body sends all of its energy into protecting you. Your thoughts race as you frantically search for the answers inside your mind, from one option to another and back again. Like a caged animal, your mind races, searching for a way out of the darkness, the situation, or the like. This is a *pivotal* moment in your journey. It is too common to become overwhelmed by this fear of the unknown, fear of the unfamiliar, and to instead choose to run back to the familiar daily life. But the past can only truly be past when you let go of the now.

When this happens, the mind can get stuck searching. But what is it that you are searching for? A light amidst the darkness to guide you. For some this light can be found during the spirit of Christmas, when spirits are lifted, gratitude is in the air, and giving is the season! It's a spark of hope. Some may call it faith. Whatever you name it doesn't matter. The only thing that matters is that you can *feel* it. That spark, that glimmer, that little tiny light you feel deep inside of you is the light you also connect to when you're in that dark tunnel. This light is not always easily tapped into. It may flicker within you from time to time, or it may shine like a stage light leading your way! The journey, my friends, is in learning to run toward that light and to let go. Letting go is a concept that took me many trials to learn. I didn't know what it was I had to let go of. You're not actually holding onto anything physical, but the energy it takes to be in a state of survival limits your ability to attract anything new.

Letting go is allowing your mind to rest. It's allowing yourself to not solve the problem, to not worry 24/7, but to be in the present moment with nothing else on your mind but the *now*. As a person with anxiety and overwhelming feelings, this sounded like a great but foreign concept.

This letting go was a process. It took many months of hell, many days of fighting with myself to even have the energy to get out of bed and face the day. When you're fighting a battle inside your head, the rest of the life process can seem overwhelming sometimes. It is important, however, to remember that you're in your head, and grounding into your physical body is important. I began this process through traditional therapy, yoga and meditation practice, and mindful nature walks. This daily practice of grounding became a part of my life and routine. Taking a hike in nature each day brought me a feeling of peace, as my body craved this time of peace and letting go. I definitely was not aware of it at the time. But that's the beauty of mindful hiking: you drop into the present moment when you're curious about a bug/flower/leaf. For a moment, you're allowing your mind to have a break and lean into the universe to support you at that time. As you learn that you can let it go, you don't need to continue to search for answers. Your energy will shift, and as it does, what you attract shifts as well.

Learning to trust in this energy, to let it go and allow it in can take a lifetime or a moment. It's all your choice. Let me help spark that light of hope inside of you, I promise, whatever it is you're dreaming of, you *can* accomplish it!

About Racquelle

Racquelle Davis (formerly Pakutz) is the founder and president of Zen Freight Solutions Inc. She is also a mentor, a bestselling author, and a mindful hiking guide. After gaining more than a decade of experience in logistics, learning the ups and downs and rights and wrongs, she chose to leave the corporate world to focus on her health, family, and quality of life. This marked the start of her entrepreneurial journey with Zen Freight Solutions and a new way of life, including healthy living, mindfulness, and self-love. She constantly strives to grow and evolve herself and develop her portfolio of knowledge every day with continual education in leadership, customer experience, and mindfulness.

As a resilient, independent woman, she leads her team and her life with faith, love, and grace. She has an insatiable drive for continuous improvement and personal development. Racquelle enjoys traveling the United States to network, visit valuable partners, and explore hiking trails along the way.

Founded in June of 2019, Zen Freight Solutions Inc. is a certified woman-owned company. Racquelle and the Zen team

Steps to Success

have helped over one hundred companies from start-ups to established transportation departments with stress-free shipping. Their mission is to continually make the transportation industry better in everything they do. They do this with a friendly voice, transparent communication, and a willingness to go above and beyond!

www.stressfreeshipping.us
linkedin.com/in/racquelle-pakutz
https://www.facebook.com/HealthyHappyHiker/

Grandma's Five Simple Steps to Success

Sandra Dawe

When I was growing up, my paternal grandmother always talked to me about responsibility. Her lessons have stuck with me. I taught them to my children when I was younger, and now, I also teach them to leaders all over the world. Everything I do started with her five simple steps to success. She never gave me an exact list to follow, but I summarized her teachings:

Grandma Padilla's Five Simple Steps to Success:

1. **You must be determined.** Go look for a job until you find one, and remember you're not too good for any job in this world.
2. **You must be reliable.** Show up early every day ready for work, even when you are sick.
3. **You must be consistent.** There are no lazy days. Do your best or more every day. Have a good attitude, even when you don't want to, and never, ever complain.
4. **You must be a hard worker.** Work harder than anyone else on your team all the time, not just when someone is watching.
5. **You must be a fast learner.** Pay attention and learn everything you can so you can be the boss one day. When you are the boss, you will know you made it in this world.

My grandmother's opinion meant the world to me, and it set the tone for my career. I earned my first director of sales and marketing role at twenty-nine, with no college degree, just experience and a couple of years as a top-ranking salesperson.

These simple steps set me apart and got me the promotions that led to my leadership role, but they didn't teach me what to do once I got there.

While I was successful in my first role and made an impact on the team I managed, I was burnt out. I didn't know how to create these qualities in the tougher team members I inherited. So, after working three hundred sixty-five days a year for three years straight, I made a new plan. I decided to quit my job and go to nursing school. I promised my husband and children I would never go back into leadership. I was wrong. Almost exactly eight years after my nursing school graduation, I was the new director of nursing and chief nursing officer for a job I loved. I inherited a complete dumpster fire, but in less than a year we improved outcomes in patient care and shifted our work culture completely. I was even nominated for Nurse Leader of the Year within my first eight months. But this job is where I learned that good employees don't leave good companies—they leave poor leaders. I could not stay without major changes happening, no matter how much I loved the people or the job. Change didn't come, so I created change—I left.

This journey brought many aha moments, but I think the biggest one was that my grandmother's five simple steps didn't work past either of my promotions into leadership. As a leader, I inherited another leader's failed or abandoned opportunities. If I heard "But this is how we've always done it" one more time, I thought I'd scream out loud, not just in my head. In my new role, I was constantly putting out fires, being interrupted while trying to focus on tasks, listening to complaints, covering call-ins, wasting time in meetings that could be e-mails, and fixing problems I didn't create and that didn't require me to fix them. And according to my employees, husband, and kids, I was working way too many hours.

In my new role, I knew that there had to be a better way. So I took a quiet, long weekend and created one. I asked three questions: What does my team need from me? What do our clients need from all of us? What do I need from my team? The team needed to be heard, seen, and appreciated, and they needed to feel supported. Our clients were the same, but they wanted to heal quickly and get back home to their responsibilities. I needed a clear vision that worked for everyone, a statement of purpose that met every need, and I needed to be less reactive and more proactive. If not, I was going to go down with the sinking ship.

I decided that weekend that I needed to do this while being me and only me, not who they wanted me to be or who they were all unintentionally asking me to be. I wrote out a plan, put it into place, and shifted the energy in one week. I thought to myself that this was just a good week, but months later, the team was still thriving, and everything had changed. Our teams were communicating, taking risks, laughing more, and working together, and our patient satisfaction scores reflected the change. I was feeling relief and could finally see a light at the end of the tunnel.

That's when an unexpected and unpredictable change came, and I was given a new leader. I worked hard to make things work, but no matter how hard we tried, we just didn't see eye to eye. I had gone from being on a high to feeling defeated. So, I went back to Grandma's simple rules, and in a moment of clarity, I knew my new task was to prevent this from happening to other leaders like me who cared.

I wanted to teach every leader what I had done, so I made another plan—a business plan. My goal is for no employee to feel the way I felt and for no leader to get burnt out and leave leadership. My new purpose was to be the unofficial leader I needed for every leader all over the world. I wanted to be a mentor, so I became a leadership instructor to send a ripple effect into workplaces across the world. My nursing knowledge backed this calling and put urgency into my actions. I knew that my stressful relationship with my own leader had affected my health and my family dynamics, and, most of all, I watched it affect my team. This is unacceptable, yet it happens in many workplaces.

When I started teaching other leaders, I remembered the values my grandmother instilled in me and started there. The training I offer is customized, but I built it off of her five basic and simple rules, only with my own unique spin:

1. **You must be determined.** Leadership is hard, but you were chosen for this role. Dig in, stay patient, and use the skills you learn to earn trust and loyalty.
2. **You must be reliable.** Your team needs you to show up for them, to advocate for them, and to lead them in every interaction.
3. **You must be consistent.** Your vision and purpose are the answers to every problem that arises and will fix every issue that comes forward. Stay proactive, not reactive.
4. **You must be a hard worker.** But we must work smarter in everything we do. Encourage your employees to speak up, to be creative, to take risks.
5. **You must be a fast learner.** Watch more than you direct and listen more than you talk. When you talk, give praise.

My grandmother's simple steps were perfect, and now her words are echoed in my teaching plans. She worked in a grocery store her whole career, and still today, she is changing workplaces.

I invite you to learn more about my story in my part memoir, part leadership book, *From Boss to Leader*. You can also set up a meeting with me to learn more about my courses or my leadership mentor group.

It's time to break the barriers that hold your team back, build bridges toward success, and find the leader that lives inside of you—the one your team has been waiting for and that this world needs.

About Sandra

Sandra Dawe has been in leadership for over thirteen years. She is a certified holistic practitioner, registered nurse, neurosciences brain specialist, leadership coach, and author of multiple books including *From Boss to Leader* and the long-anticipated *Reckless Abandon*, due to release in 2025. She empowers individuals by teaching them how chronic stress, relationships, and their careers affect long-term health outcomes.

Sandra's leadership courses are customized to help people enhance communication, foster trust, and reshape workplace cultures. Through her work, she inspires leaders to set clear visions, break barriers that hold people back, and find the true leader who lives inside of them. Her mission is to create a global ripple effect of positive change that follows every employee and leader home, creating a healthier and happier world.

Steps to Success

To learn more, visit www.sandradawe.com or email her at sandra@sandradawe.com.

You Want Me to What?

Jackee Ging

When you're starting a new position at an established company, changing industries, or perhaps being crazy enough to start your own venture, you may find yourself in unfamiliar territory. Being uncomfortable can become your new norm. But it doesn't have to be that way.

Many people are in jobs/positions where they wonder, *How did I end up here*? You grow up and go to school thinking you will go into a certain field or dream about a very specific position. You might only be aware of a small sample of opportunities and have no clue what else is available or suitable for you. Then, through luck, determination, strategy, perseverance, or a combination of all, you end up doing something in a field you never imagined.

There are so many possibilities out there. You can't even begin to imagine the industries and opportunities that are available to you. For example, while I was an advertising salesperson for a professional trade organization, I never imagined I'd be going to a conference entitled, "World of Concrete!" And what a world it was! At the time, it was one of the largest conventions in the country; only New Orleans and Las Vegas had facilities large enough to host the indoor-outdoor convention. While I became familiar with the world of coatings and all that it entailed, this was only a small sliver of concrete industries.

I only point this out to show that there are so many fields that are different worlds to so many people! And you can make any of them your world.

When I became an entrepreneur (not something I'd ever imagined, planned, or dreamed about) someone wiser than me told me, "You get what you focus on." I'd heard that many times before but never really listened or took the words to heart. At this time, being out on my own, with no one to set the parameters, I learned that you have to envision what you want and make that your sole mission.

Sometimes you get to a point where you're more cautious than usual. Sometimes you need a nudge to move forward. It could be procrastination. It could be nerves. It could be that you're a perfectionist. Whatever the reason, in the words of a certain shoe company—*Just do it!*

Back when I was a consultant, I was creating business and marketing plans for clients. Doing one for myself, however, was a different story. As a solo entrepreneur, you only have one person to assign the "to-do's" to, and many of these might be out of your normal wheelhouse. Most people will do the things they do well or are familiar with first. But what about the tough parts of the job? To get up and running, you can't have excuses. If you wait for things to be perfect, it's never going to get done. Rip the Band-Aid off, do it to the best of your ability, and move forward. The key is that you learned what you needed to in order to get it done and that you'll be able to do it better the next time. Starting on your own isn't for the faint of heart.

Marketing (in any form) and communications are the building blocks to almost any position, whether you realize it or not. Marketing can be a phone call, a post, or simply an introduction. Marketing channels have changed a lot in the past thirty years. Gone are the dark ages of hovering over a fax machine or mailing press releases. How did we manage? The ability to google and to have a boatload of information at your fingertips in mere seconds only accelerates the steps. The basics are the basics. (Is that similar to "the standard is the standard"?) Without the ability to create recognition or buzz, your position or company will either falter or become stale.

So what basics can you do if you are a one-man show, or if you simply believe you don't have that marketing gene in you?

Most people have heard about the seven "Ps" of marketing: product, price, promotion, place, people, packaging, and process. But that can sound intimidating. If you are just starting out, you have your product or service, and chances are you know your pricing and have figured that out early. "Promotion" and "people" go together as you need to plan (possibly another "P"?) your promotions. "People" refers to anyone who comes in contact with your product/good or service. Basic networking is an efficient way to accomplish this without a lot of investment.

You wouldn't be reading this book if you didn't already know that networking was good for you. Similar to medicine, you might do it only to change an existing situation or when forced to do it. The thing is, networking doesn't have to be torture. The key is the opposite of what you might think. Yes, you need to be prepared with a simplified pitch in the back of your mind (i.e., be able to clearly answer what you do and what sets you apart from your competitors), but a successful networker is a good *listener*. When you attend a professional organization's meeting or go to a networking luncheon, it doesn't have to be torture. Many introverts would rather poke out their eyes, but if you have faith in your product or service, these opportunities shouldn't be avoided. Ask open-ended questions that facilitate conversation. People want to know that you have heard and appreciate their experience and what they have to say. Be patient and learn about your new contact. Maybe they won't become your new BFF and have no interest in knowing what you want to tell them, but there's a chance one of their contacts or BFFs could be a potential link or match for your product or service. Networking is about building relationships, not just making contacts.

I have also learned the power of being a connector or intermediary. At any networking event, there can be people from a wide range of industries. You might get to an event and realize it isn't your audience. Rather than calling it a night, however, try to make at least one new contact. If you ask questions and learn about others, you might be able to connect them to their ideal customer. At the very least, you can do them a favor and hook them up with someone who can be advantageous to them. Chances are strong that you will be remembered, and that person, in turn, will try to return the favor!

If, by chance, you have made a new contact that could become a client/customer, don't give away the store! Save something for the second date. Leave them wanting more! Follow-up can be what sets you apart. A simple thank-you email could separate you from the pack. Share links to websites that might interest them, or send an article that reflects something you discussed. Initially, it doesn't have to be about you. Find common ground, and build a relationship. Then you can begin to sell or market. Zig Ziglar, bestselling author and motivational speaker, said, "If people like you they will listen to you, but if they trust you they'll do business with you." Understanding others' needs by listening will certainly help you in the long run.

Making connections online can be an effective networking strategy. But it shouldn't be your only one. In the post-COVID era, there has been a return to in-person meetings. And although it can be intimidating and one of your least favorite tasks or to-dos, networking shouldn't be avoided.

Networking can help your business grow because it can connect you with a variety of indirect leads, help generate new ideas, and increase your visibility. Some of the most successful people I know have a very eclectic network. When you develop a new contact, you are a step closer to their network. In one of my favorite networking groups for entrepreneurs, we used to say that we became each other's board of directors. As a group, we could refer you to almost any professional you might need.

It's difficult to quantify successful networking. It's all about planting seeds. The hardest part is going in cold. That said, having a plan and knowing your basic lines should remove the intimidation factor. Maintaining these relationships can be a full-time job in itself. But if you are lucky enough, the people you meet via networking may just become your friends. And years down the road, you might end up being a part of an anthology with them!

Unfortunately, there's no getting around it. Success, in any part of life, isn't easy. Getting out of your comfort zone is a must. Being uncomfortable, whether you're exploring unknown industries or doing a one-eighty on your career path, can ultimately change your life. After all, I never would've thought I'd know anything about industrial coatings (that's what I used to call "paint"), changing sparkplugs, or driving a box truck. You never know what that next road will be!

About Jackee

Jackee Ging is a project coordinator at Schneider Electric and owns the mobile boutique Style Truck, which was named Boutique of the Year at Style Week Pittsburgh in 2015. She specializes in marketing, business development, and communications for startups and small businesses and brings over twenty-five years of experience in corporate marketing and sales coordination.

Before becoming an entrepreneur in 2012, Jackee was a consultant for ADAPT Solutions, focusing on new business development, sales, and marketing within the industrial sector. She has also held positions as a relocation consultant and marketing business development manager. Her favorite job, however, has been dog walker.

Currently, Jackee serves as the marketing chair on the board of Prostate Cancer Pittsburgh and is the president of her church's Women's Guild. She graduated with a marketing degree from Grove City College and obtained a professional writing certificate from Robert Morris University. Follow her online: www.facebook.com/styletruck or www.instagram.com/mystyletruck/. Or visit www.mystyletruck.com.

Combat Boots

Christina Keener

"Never give up, never give up, never give up."
~ Winston Churchill

"If you ever feel like quitting, remember why you started in the first place." This is a quote I read as I was shuffling along the formation line collecting my supplies during the reception process before basic training. The quote was written with a black Sharpie on a cut-out piece of cardboard, taped to a register that wasn't exactly going to ring us up for purchase. A civilian woman stood ready to tell us which direction to go with our pile of PT (physical training) clothing and army-green duffle bags.

If you're not familiar with the reception battalion, picture a place like Allegheny County Prison and MedExpress combined. You have the strict drill sergeants giving you one last chance to turn in any contraband (aka, forbidden items), illegal items, etc., otherwise known as the "shakedown." Then you're shuffled from one building to the next to have physicals, administrative background checks, and shots. Yes, lots of shots and miscellaneous medication. Still today I don't know what I ingested.

I thought to myself, *Quitting?* How could a thought like that cross my mind? I survived a divorce after ten years of marriage, worked my way up to becoming an accounting manager for a million-dollar steel company, and made it here to accomplish my goal of joining the military. Thinking back to that quote gave me a sense of pride. I don't quit. I am a mentally strong woman who has encountered hardship and survived. I clung to that quote over the next few days (yes, days) as I embarked on one of the most physically demanding challenges of my life.

Steps to Success

I read a book during my divorce called *13 Things Mentally Strong People Don't Do* by Amy Morin. The author talked about her personal struggle with loss and grief and the experiences she had with clients as a licensed therapist. With her personal experience and professional acumen, she wrote thirteen virtues that essentially help you become mentally stronger. That book gave me the mental fortitude to accept a new life of being single, manage my emotions, and have confidence in myself to make mature decisions not just about what I felt. It was this maturity and mental strength that gave me the courage to call the army recruiter in November 2022.

Here I was, standing outside of the building with the other female trainees with our duffle bags filled with supplies, PT uniforms, and PT shoes. I listened to how tomorrow we would be issued our OCPs (operational camouflage pattern uniforms) and combat boots. Our OCPs—now I would feel like a real soldier.

"Y'all got baby feet," the black male drill sergeant said to the female trainees as we stood in line waiting to get our issued combat boots. He was rubbing his fingertips into his palm to emphasize how soft our feet were. "It will take some time for your feet to callus and adjust to wearing these," he said. The South Carolina heat quickly crept up on us, and to my relief, the drill sergeant ordered all of us to enter the air-conditioned building to get our assigned combat boots. The other females and I were assigned to a platoon, otherwise known as a "group" or "unit" in military terms. There were twelve to twenty females all coming from different backgrounds—White, Black, Asian, and Hispanic—from different parts of the country and the world. I remember some of the younger females who were in awe that they were beside a thirty-seven-year-old woman. I was mistaken many times for being in my twenties, so I often heard, "You're thirty-seven?!" or "My mom is the same age as you!"

After two days of the newly assigned boots and the South Carolina, July humidity in full swing, I felt miserable. I couldn't adjust to standing in formation for hours at a time while the sun beat down on us. It frustrated me that we (i.e., our platoon and any trainee in the reception area) were getting yelled at to stand up straight, drink water, don't sleep, clean the barracks, etc. The list went on and on. Worst of all, my feet hurt. I mean *really* hurt. It felt like someone was jamming needles into my heels and the balls of my feet, and the only relief I had was to sit down. I even tried switching to my PT shoes in the hopes that some relief would come as I walked around, and even that didn't help.

Waiting in line for the chow hall first brought suffering then comfort. The chow hall was a giant, make-shift white tent (just like the circus) that housed all the cooking staff, equipment, buffet lines, and tables for all the trainees at reception. No exaggeration, it would take over an hour of standing outside to move each trainee through the line to enter the tent. Did you ever go to an amusement park with a really long wait anticipating the ride? That's how I felt each time I was about to eat, only I was in agony while I waited. Then I'd have a sense of relief for roughly twelve to fifteen minutes while selecting my food and then sitting down to eat to my heart's glory. Despite the agony of standing and all the strenuous rules, the army did feed us well, and I never left the chow hall hungry.

As we were dismissed from lunch and sent outside to stand in formation *again*, trainees learned when to scope out for drill sergeants. They either wore their OCPs, along with their infamous, green drill sergeant hats, or their PT uniforms with neon-looking safety vests labeled "Drill Sergeant." If there was no drill sergeant in sight, we knew we could sit down! It was just enough if I could give my feet some relief for a few minutes before we were off marching and standing again. After all, if they can't see us, then it must be okay, right? There's a cadence we would sing that would go, "Everywhere I gooooo, there's a drill sergeant there!"

Well, our few minutes of sitting was quickly interrupted when a Hispanic female drill sergeant appeared outside to see dozens of her trainees were sitting. Her words were a loud wake-up call: "All you have to do is stand!" she hollered at the platoons. "Your bones are so weak, you can't even stand! You're all used to sitting at home and playing video games. This is what the army sends us? Are any of you old enough to remember 9/11?!"

Whew. Those words stung. I remembered 9/11. It happened when I was in tenth grade. I remembered that yearning feeling I had in my dining room when I twenty-seven, thinking what it would be like to be in the army. I remembered why I swore in and took my oath in May 2023. I remembered why I was here. Sure, the pain in my feet was bothering me, but I had to channel the strength within myself and say, "Keep going, one day at a time. Just one more day!"

One of the supplies we received was the *Basic Training Handbook*, which covers army history, the song, the soldiers' creed, tips for personal hygiene, ranks, pay grades, and personal development. One of the subjects asks: What is one goal or challenge that you would like to overcome? I grabbed some loose-leaf paper and jotted down the challenges I was facing:

Maintaining the pain in my feet
Handling the heat and humidity of South Carolina
Building the endurance to stand in formation without feeling tired

As days went by, it didn't feel like any relief was coming to my feet, body, or mindset. But I believe all the prayers from my family, friends, and church moved me each day to keep going and push through the day. My biggest fear was creeping up on me because, if my feet hurt this bad at reception, how was I going to get through basic training? A typical timeframe for reception can take four to seven days. However, because I came through on what was called a "summer surge," the barracks were backed up at basic training, and the trainees were forced to wait there for almost two weeks. Even though I felt this agony for roughly two weeks, when the time came for all the trainees to pack up and move on to the barracks for basic training, I was ready. I'll never forget stepping off that white prison-like bus, my feet finally callused and the sweltering pain gone. I believe that because I'd spent so much time standing and waiting, my bones could finally withstand all that standing.

Fast-forward through thirteen weeks of strenuous training, obstacle courses, ruck marches, a diagnosis of pneumonia and the flu (another huge setback that caused me to become hospitalized and "recycled" to another battalion for an additional three weeks outside of the ten-week training)...those same combat boots that caused me so much misery led me to victory by completing the infamous, ten-mile ruck march known as "The Forge."

I've always wondered if whoever wrote that quote on the cardboard back in reception ever thought how many trainees would cling to it as much as I did. I look back now and remember the thought of quitting, but I also remember why I started in the first place.

About Christina

When Christina Keener was twenty-seven years old, she imagined what it would be like to join the U.S. Army and serve her nation. After earning a bachelor of accounting degree from the University of Phoenix, she started working as a staff accountant at a hospitality company. She attended a Toastmasters meeting and quickly formed a bond with the members. Through speeches and feedback, Christina overcame her shyness and no longer felt like the "quiet accountant" in the cubical. Although joining the army was on her mind, it didn't seem like the right time to enlist, and she worried that she missed the cutoff age.

Ten years later, Christina experienced the hardships of a divorce but persisted in the field of accounting and persevered as an accounting manager for an international steel company. By thirty-seven, she realized she didn't want to live with regret and decided to pursue her dream of becoming a U.S. soldier. As fate would have it, the army raised the entrance age to thirty-nine in 2022, allowing her to make an appointment with a recruiter.

Christina combined her love of food and her passion for the military by enlisting as a U.S. Army Reservist as a 92G Culinary Specialist. She completed basic training and advanced individual training at an age when soldiers could retire. When she's not crunching numbers at her civilian job or feeding hungry soldiers at the unit, Christina enjoys spending time with her family and friends, reading, shopping, trying new dishes, and traveling to exotic destinations. Her favorite quote, read by a professor at her undergrad ceremony in 2012, is "Don't let your emotions get in the way of your intellect."

https://www.facebook.com/christina.keener.3/
https://www.linkedin.com/in/christina-keener-dtm-7576a2191/

A Winning Mistake

Joy Klohonatz

Have you ever made a silly, honest mistake and totally beat yourself up for it? One where you just shake your head and wonder, *how in the world did I do that?*

That was me twelve years ago. I didn't know it was a mistake that would lead me to what I feel is my purpose in this life today.

I had a successful twenty-three-year career in retail management for a large, growing store chain. I was recruited right out of college, worked my way up, and became one of the first of seven women to ever manage this retail giant. Eventually, I got married and began to raise two children. I soon realized that a twelve-to-fourteen-hour-day career was not as rewarding anymore, and I chose to step down.

This launched me into a world of volunteerism and entrepreneurship. A few years later, we relocated to another state for my husband's career. After my children got acclimated to the new area and in the schools, I felt the need to do something for myself while contributing to the family income. I found a network marketing home party plan company with products and a mission I truly believed in, and I launched on a journey of personal development, positive energy, gratitude, and of course, fun.

During this time, I was introduced to a unique system to thank my customers and hostesses at a higher level. This little online greeting card system added another layer of uniqueness where I could express my appreciation to others with written words, messages and photos. The hostesses loved that I took the time to capture those moments and thanked them with a tangible card with photos of their friends.

Steps to Success

After six years, out of the blue, this home party plan company announced it was going to close. Two months later, I felt lost again.

As I was licking my wounds of disappointment and exploring what to do next, and with the holidays coming, I decided to use this greeting card system to send my personal holiday cards. Although I was a monthly subscriber, I still needed to purchase more cards to complete my list. I didn't know it then, but instead of just purchasing a few extra cards, I had resubscribed. I hadn't caught it on my credit card statements yet so it was quite a surprise when I did a month later.

So, what did I do? Instead of continuing to beat myself up, I realized that the Easter-Lenten season was happening over the next forty days and decided I was going to send three random cards a day to different people. A word of gratitude, congratulations, celebration, inspiration, or just simply, "thinking about you."

I started with my book of contacts. Then I began listening differently to conversations and becoming more aware of marketing signs that celebrated people. In fact, one time our local Wendy's restaurant was celebrating an employee of the month, and I sent a congratulations card to her at the restaurant. I found out later that her manager recognized her in front of the rest of the other employees which set off a ripple effect of recognition.

It was a fun forty days; however, I was not prepared for the impact I was really making. I received many phone calls, texts, and emails of thanks and appreciation. I even had two people call me in tears about how bad a day they were having until they went to their mailbox and opened my card. People felt noticed, cared about, and appreciated.

This was my aha moment. I knew I had something special here, and I felt I needed to pursue it more. I found out that the card company had a business opportunity, and although I didn't understand all the mechanics, I knew how to make people feel good, and that was good enough for me.

I am a person who, once I decide to commit, I am all in. So when I heard this company was having a Treat-em-Right seminar in Florida (I'm in Pennsylvania), I knew I had to get there, but at the time, paying the hotel price was tough. I connected with a fellow consultant who offered me a couch in her camper with her and her dog. It would be the first time we ever met, but it didn't stop me, and off I went! And I was so glad I did.

I had been introduced to personal development teachings in the past but not to the extent that I learned with this little card company. I was a bit uncomfortable with everything, at first, but felt the connection and comfort of those around me. The founder and all the people in attendance had one big thing in common: they believed in the power of gratitude and were determined to tell the world about it. I heard these words that have stuck with me today: "Life is not promised to any of us, so we need to celebrate people while they are here, not when they are gone."

This aligned with me, knowing that one of the most important emotions people need today is the need to feel loved and appreciated. I felt so blessed to have found a way to do this consistently. I write *gratitude is everything* in my journal daily because it is.

There is good and bad social media today, but focusing on the good allows you to see what is important in other people's lives. Being able to capture those moments and send back to them a tangible card that they can touch, feel, and read repeatedly preserves that moment for them. And that is special.

I get calls and messages almost daily expressing not just thanks but how the card touched them in a special way. I rarely attend an event where someone doesn't come up to me and thank me for a card I sent them. People frame them, put them on their fridges, and carry them with them. One time I even had someone ask if I could send them another card because the first one had gotten worn out.

I have to share this special moment:

Once traveling through a small town, my husband got stopped going a bit too fast. Luckily, he just got a warning. I felt it would be nice to send the officer a thank you. So, I did along with a Starbucks gift card. I never expected to hear anything back, but one day, an envelope from the State Police arrived. After expressing how rarely a police officer gets such a message and thanking me for the gift card (even though he gave it back, as they aren't allowed to receive gifts), these last words touched me: "I kept the 'thank you' card and will place it with the other mementos of my career that will be passed on to my children."

WOW! I am part of his legacy!

I tell people all the time, whether I'm receiving an income or not, I would still send these heartfelt cards because I know the positive impact they make. I can't claim that I'm changing the world one card at a time (clichéd, I know), but I *can* claim that I am changing a moment for that one person.

It's always a blessing when I can speak in front of groups of people about this mission of gratitude. Even if some don't grasp the simplicity of the power, they have to make a difference, I know I am in the right place for those who do. I smile up at my mom when I hear the words, "Joy, your mom sure gave you the perfect name."

I love my journaling as I start and end each day with what I am grateful for. I see the world differently and feel the need to give back more. I contribute to several philanthropic groups, but my proudest is leading a philanthropic group of women whose sole purpose is to help other women and children have better lives. Together we have been able to make an impact of over $95,000!

Today I am blessed beyond measure for what I have been given. I am doing something that is making a difference in a world, where eighty percent of what we hear is negative. I am giving people hope and purpose. It has connected me to a higher purpose, and I didn't even know I needed it. When you live in gratitude every single day, more things present themselves to be grateful for. Can you imagine a world where everyone lived like this every day?

One of my favorite quotes that I think of often is from the late Maya Angelou: "I've learned that people will forget what you said, people will forget what you did, but people will never forget how you made them feel."[1]

About Joy

---

[1] 2004, The Arts Go To School: Classroom-based activities that focus on music, painting, drama, movement, media, and more, Edited by David Booth and Masayuki Hachiya, (Sidebar quotation), Quote Page 14, Published by Pembroke Publishers, Markham, Ontario, Distributed by Stenhouse Publishers, Portland, Maine. (Verified on paper)

Joy is currently a gratitude consultant with Promptings, recently earning the rank of Platinum and is honored to be serving on the prestigious Eagles Nest advisory board.

Joy knows that appreciating and celebrating people in all aspects of their lives is the key to a fulling and successful life. Graduating from Penn State University with a degree in retail management led her to become one of the first of seven women to become a general store manager of K-marts, and she received many awards for superior customer service and employee retention.

Joy's heart is always about making a difference in others' lives, and this is reflected in her continued philanthropic work. She is the chapter leader for Inspired Women Paying it Forward - Westmoreland County, which has awarded over $95,000 to nonprofits benefiting women and girls locally and globally. She is also a founding member of Angela's Angels and volunteers with United Women with United Way of Southwest Pennsylvania.

Joy has been recognized for numerous awards such as BPW Woman of the Year, Volunteer of the Year, and Chamber Ambassador. In 2023, she was honored with the coveted ATHENA Award in Westmoreland County, Pa.

Joy is an international speaker and trainer. She loves knowing she is helping others understand the importance of making a difference because, at the end of the day, gratitude is everything.

j.klohonatz@gmail.com
www.carewithjoy.net

Surviving to Thriving

Lori Ann Lewicki

Life has not always looked so pretty. There was a time when I wasn't even sure I was going to make it. I would never have dreamed of being in the amazing place I am now.

I was involved in a car accident while in the middle of a messy divorce. I lost my job, my home. I was diagnosed with cancer and had to have surgery. To top off the stellar year I was having, I lost my mother, my only friend left in the world. That was almost twelve years ago. I was broken and alone, but I always had faith that my life would get better. I started reading to gain perspective. I started investing in my own mental health. I started connecting with women who were where I wanted to be in life so I could elevate my own. It has been a journey of self-love, self-discovery, and self-expression.

I have been a registered nurse for many years and have always helped others heal. This was new territory for me: healing myself.

Being a nurse was all I knew; it was so far out of my comfort zone to label myself as anything other than a nurse. It felt so awkward to say I was going to be an author. I started telling everyone that I was going to write a book because I wanted to hold myself accountable.

My line-in-the-sand moment happened about two years ago. I had been saying for years that I needed to write my book and start a life-coaching business. I had been working with my own life coach for several years, growing and expanding each year. One day, my coach had a guest speaker in the group who did a birth chart reading, and she explained that by telling my story, I was connecting to my higher purpose in life. I was still feeling inadequate, however, and I would get that sinking feeling of

Steps to Success

"Who wants to read about me?" It's the feeling of being an imposter. I was afraid no one would take me seriously as a coach. I let my fears hold me back for another few months until I spoke with my friend Cori about what her program entailed and how writing a book would work. This was uncharted territory for me. I was so intimidated by the whole process, but Cori's encouraging words pierced through my heart like a dagger.

I finally took my dreams seriously when I hired Cori as my writing coach. I knew I needed someone to hold me accountable to finish the book, but it wasn't until a couple of weeks into working together, during one of our sessions, that Cori said something that rocked me to my core. We had been working on which stories needed to be in my book and what could be left out. At this point, she knew most of my story, how traumatic it was, and how I learned and grew into the person I am today. Then she said the pivotal words that sparked a fire inside of me: "Your story is going to be someone else's survival guide."

Those words cut through me. They struck deeply to my core. My years of being a nurse taught me that we are trained to give of ourselves to our patients. Up until that moment, I had put in the bare minimum into my new business adventure, but now, I felt empowered not only to write my book to the best of my ability, but to truly invest in myself. This was such a pivotal moment in my life. I started *believing* that my story was going to help other nurses unlike anything out there. I started *believing* that my mess of a life could be turned into a message that God was going to use for his good. I live to serve others. Helping people makes my soul happy. That was the moment my life changed. I was so excited to start writing. I was still scared about the new adventure I was embarking on but also elated that my pain could be used for good in the world. If my story only helps one person, it will all have been worth it.

Writing my story was so healing. It was such an amazing experience to release so much hurt that I didn't realize I was still holding on to. I have grown my group by hundreds and even opened it up to anyone who wants to be encouraged and loved. I have gotten many messages from other nurses who I have helped love their careers again. I have been told that I inspired someone to reopen their business because that's where their passion was. I inspired another to design her book. I had one nurse tell me she was going to write *her* story to help inspire other nurses who have a similar story. I created a masterclass on self-care. I wrote an article about preventing burnout and signed on to author another chapter in a third book. I am a life coach for nurses. I have also collaborated with a fellow nurse executive who wants to make a bigger impact on the nursing profession.

All these things would never have happened if I had not been bold enough to take a chance on myself. Loving who you are for what you have experienced is a life lesson worth figuring out.

While I am still a nurse because I love caring for others, I am also integrating my coaching into my way of life. I have more confidence to embrace life. All the shame and regret I was holding inside for so long has been lifted by telling my story. I was able to shine a light on all the dark spots of my character. Life is exhilarating again. I bought a Harley Davidson as a gift to myself for sticking with the hard parts and publishing my story, and that has led to an unprecedented amount of confidence. Now, I am ready to conquer the world of public speaking and life coaching to impact as many people as I can.

About Lori

Lori Ann Lewicki is an ICU travel nurse, life and health coach for nurses, wife, mother of four (ages 26, 24, 19 and 3), and daughter of a Vietnam veteran—so she never gets a day off from being a nurse. She is also an advocate for living your dreams.

Writing her first book, *Surviving Shit Creek*, empowered Lori to follow her own dreams. Because she has grown so much as a nurse and a human, she hopes to inspire others to go after their dreams and never quit learning to be better than the day before.

Lori is a holistic healer who believes everyone has the ability to thrive. She graduated from Community College of Allegheny County with her ADN in nursing in 2004 and, being a nerd, also graduated with an associate's degree in psychology. She obtained her BSN in 2006 from California University of Penn., her PHRN in 2010, had her first CCRN from 2007–2010, her MSN in 2022, and retested for her CCRN in 2024. Lori has also been a certified health coach since 2019. She has worked in the ICU, in the ER, on the ambulance, in medical review, in home care, and as a nursing instructor over her career, for more than 20 years.

One of Lori's dreams was to buy a Harley and get her motorcycle license, which she did in celebration of the completion of *Surviving Shit Creek*.

I Could Never Do That... or Can I?

Beth Sanchez

I love watching superhero origin stories. Every hero has an origin story. For that matter, every person has an origin story, even you and me. I like to think I can be somebody's hero through my company's Impactful Improv programs. While my hero's journey is still in its early stages, my origin story serves as the foundation for my success as a business owner.

Journey Begins with Childhood Dreams

My story begins with dreams planted during my childhood. My Minnie Mouse doll was my constant companion. My dad would take me on father-daughter dates to see the latest Disney film, followed by dinner at McDonald's. As adolescence set in, I outgrew my love of Disney, or so I thought. When Disney released animated classics like *Cinderella* on home video, my passion was reignited. I studied not only the animated classics but also Walt Disney as a person and the company that endures as his legacy. By the time I entered college, the dream was clear: I wanted to work for the Walt Disney Company as an executive one day. As it turned out, that dream would serve as a catalyst for my journey to a higher purpose.

Walt Disney World College Program

My first major step toward a Disney career came in 1996 when I was accepted to the Walt Disney World College Program and earned my "Ducktorate" from Disney University. In addition to networking and learning about the company, I enjoyed the experience of living at Disney. One night a week, cast members (Disney's term for employees) could visit the Pleasure Island nighttime entertainment complex for free. It was so much fun exploring all the themed clubs. Little did I know that one of those clubs, the Comedy Warehouse, would become a pivotal step toward discovering the core of my business offering.

When I entered the Comedy Warehouse for the first time, I expected to see the one kind of comedy I knew: live stand-up. I still remember the experience clearly. Props from old Disney attractions lined the walls. We descended the stairs to take a seat behind a counter-like table to hold snacks and drinks while enjoying the show. The performers took the stage and introduced me to a new kind of comedy: improv. I laughed as they performed scenes and even musical numbers. The performers were so fluid, I couldn't believe they were making everything up on the spot! I knew there must be a plant in the audience. At one point, the audience member sitting directly behind me gave the suggestion that inspired the scene. After the show, I asked who he knew in the cast. The man said, "I'm just on vacation and have no connection." I remember being amazed by how they could create such cohesive, funny scenes without any rehearsal. *Impressive*, I thought. *But I could never do that.* For many years, I attended shows at the Comedy Warehouse and occasionally caught an episode of *Whose Line Is It Anyway?* on TV, but only for pure entertainment.

Getting Back on Track

Fast-forward to 2012. After a series of employment opportunities that detoured my journey, I decided to finally achieve my Disney dream and return to school to transition from healthcare to the entertainment industry by earning my master of business administration (MBA). My classmates remember my focus and clarity as I declared my goal to work for the Walt

Disney Company. Improv once again appeared on my path as part of our orientation. We experienced what I now call *applied improvisation* through exercises designed to help us break the ice and get to know each other as an incoming class. This was my first introduction to the multitude of life skills an improviser uses on stage, like being fully present, actively listening, and trusting fellow teammates. I cannot remember most of the exercises except the "One Word Story," where we told a hilarious story about a stapler by each contributing one word at a time. Once again, I felt this was valuable, but I thought, *I could never do that*.

The Real Journey Begins

Every hero experiences a point on their journey when a major crisis or setback occurs that makes the hero evaluate their path. I had the opportunity to work for Disney as a professional following my MBA graduation. Unfortunately, I was hired into the wrong seat on the proverbial team bus and failed miserably. Only five months into the role, I admitted defeat and resigned. The resignation marked the end of a lifelong dream and left me lost.

In every hero's journey, a teacher, often referred to as the "reflection character," comes into the hero's life to put a mirror to the hero to expose their true essence and set them on the right path. For me, a career coach I hired proved to be that guide. Instead of reviewing my resume and learning about my interests, my coach guided me through the grieving process of losing my career dream and uncovered my "creative, entrepreneurial spirit." When he suggested that I start a company applying my facilitation skills combined with applied improv, my response was, "I could never do that. Besides, there are already a growing number of improvisers who apply their craft to business." "But why can't you?" he replied. "There are plenty of opportunities, and you offer a unique business perspective based on your diverse consulting and corporate experiences."

My career coach's nudge sparked the creation of what has become the Impactful Improv program. As I developed the program, I began to study the art of improv and how to best use it as a facilitation tool. I even perform on stage with an improv team, introducing children to the fun and skills improv offers. One of the proudest moments of my life was the day I won a contract for a major consulting company over a renowned improv organization. I realized I could do this really well.

I don't know what the future holds, but I have learned to love the journey as my clients continue to inspire me to create new series and workshops to support the achievement of their goals. One of my favorite clients hired me to do a series of educational workshops and virtual team-building happy hours. At each workshop, I always start with an icebreaker name game where each person shares one word tied to a theme. We then use these words to practice the importance of both sending and receiving communication while getting to know each other. And of course, the one-word story is never the same but always generates laughter along with the reminder that, while things don't always turn out as we planned, a great story (or project) is delivered through teamwork.

The Journey Continues

My journey is just getting started. There are still ideas that frighten me, where my initial gut reaction is *I could never do that*. Thanks to the seeds planted during my journey, my brain now quickly redirects me to ask, *How can I do that?* I never dreamed I would own my own business or perform on a stage, yet here I am.

In *The Hero's Journey,* Joseph Campbell explains that the hero's story is not at the end, but rather, "...the hero comes back from this mysterious adventure with the power to bestow boons on his fellow man." It is now my turn to help others stretch beyond their comfort zones to do the things they never thought they could do, whether as a team reaching for a sales goal or an individual finding the path to their higher purpose.

So, what is one thing you never thought you could do but could improve your business or life? I challenge you to take one step to start your own hero's adventure today.

About Beth

Beth Sanchez is the founder and CEO of Impactful Improv, a company dedicated to helping professionals and teams improve critical business skills such as active listening, adaptive thinking, and collaboration. With a background in business and a passion for personal development, Beth facilitates improv-inspired workshops drawing on her wide range of corporate experiences that stretch participants beyond their comfort zones to think on their feet, improve communication, adapt quickly to change, and foster stronger team engagement—all while having fun.

Beth discovered the value of improv for skill building while earning her master of business administration at Duke University's Fuqua School of Business.

Before founding Impactful Improv, Beth worked with organizations including Accenture, The Walt Disney Company, UPMC, and Highmark, where she honed her business and leadership skills across diverse industries.

Flip the Script to Win More Referrals

Virginia Weida

The knot in my stomach was a painful reminder that I had ignored my intuition. A routine check-in call with a client on Monday morning escalated quickly, causing stress and frustration. Miscommunication had thrown a wrench into the weeks of meticulous planning, leaving crucial connections unfinished during the weekend move. Some final wiring could not be completed in the floor and, therefore, some staff would not have access to the internet until the subcontractors could return to the site. Sensing the urgency, I immediately jumped into action coordinating with technicians to get everyone back online as soon as possible. It was a stark reminder that even the most carefully laid plans can crumble, and in those moments, adapting and leaning into your strengths is paramount.

The previous week, I'd spent a great deal of time checking and double-checking with the furniture vendor, the low-voltage cabling contractor, the electrician, and the client to ensure everything was coordinated. As a workplace design expert for many years, I found this process routine and predictable. The client had coordinated the data locations and was managing the move, and they reassured me that they had everything they needed to complete the work. I still had a feeling that something was just not quite right. On Friday, I asked the client again, "Do you need me to stop by Saturday during the move?"

"Oh, no need," they replied. "We'll be fine."

I ignored my instincts telling me otherwise and planned my weekend as usual.

When the problems with the installation came to light on Saturday, tension increased and finger-pointing ensued. Those not present were getting the most blame for the issue. Could I have facilitated a solution that afternoon during the move? We won't know for sure, but at least by Monday morning I would have been a step ahead in resolving it. In hindsight, I should have listened to my gut and stopped in to visit rather than assuming everything would go according to plan, even if the move was not in my scope and I was nearing the end of my project fees. It would have still been a stressful experience, but I would have been able to reduce my client's anxiety at the moment and solve their problems, which is a key part of my service success.

I spent a great deal of time planning the plan, so to speak, yet unexpected things still came up that caused client dissatisfaction, whether they were in my purview or not. No project is perfect, of course, but I could have done better. No matter the amount of planning, an entrepreneur's journey is often full of twists, turns, and surprises. The crisis was resolved quickly that next week, but it caused a lot of frustration and delayed other work. Things needed to change for the better. So, once the situation was resolved, I reflected on all that had happened and what could be different.

Going through this and similar challenging situations early in my entrepreneurial journey forced me to reassess how to improve my project management process for clients, moving forward. I knew I could no longer do it the way it had always been done. Should I make Saturday site visits a standard procedure for my projects? What would need to change in my process to make this happen? Did I have to raise my rates, or was there some other way I could shift things around to cover my expenses for more site visits? This introspective process was not new to me, and I approached the work with a positive attitude.

Virginia Weida

My Unexpected Entrepreneurial Journey

Since college, my goal had been to lead a prestigious architectural firm's commercial interior design department. I worked hard toward that goal in the first part of my career, prioritizing work and spending many long hours on projects. When it was finally within my grasp, however, I changed gears to start my own company. Why did I do that when I'd finally achieved my biggest goal? It was not a quick decision; it had been coming for several years. It turned out that the reality of what I had thought I wanted all along was no longer right for me.

In 2006, instead of accepting a shareholder agreement, I became an entrepreneur and set new goals for my professional path. As I worked on a business plan and set marketing goals, I looked for ways to improve processes and stand apart from the competition. How could I best differentiate myself? What could I change or modify to improve project outcomes and client satisfaction? Could I flip the script to win more customers?

I work in the commercial real estate industry as a workplace design expert. Many procedures must be followed in my industry, as we affect people's health, safety, and well-being. A large part of the undergraduate education for interior designers is spent on training procedures and requirements for the construction industry. I'm sure anyone in the medical, insurance, financial, legal, and other similar fields can relate. Yet, one of the joys of owning your own business is creating change and trying new ideas. How can an entrepreneur possibly do this in such a restricted field? We can start by looking at the bigger picture.

Steps to Success

Project Success Cycle, With a Twist

No matter the industry, all business success follows a similar overall process: marketing, planning, executing, closing out, and then repeating the cycle. For businesses that offer a service, your particular project may be designing and building a new home for a client, finding new customers to come to your bakery, or gaining new clientele for your beauty salon.

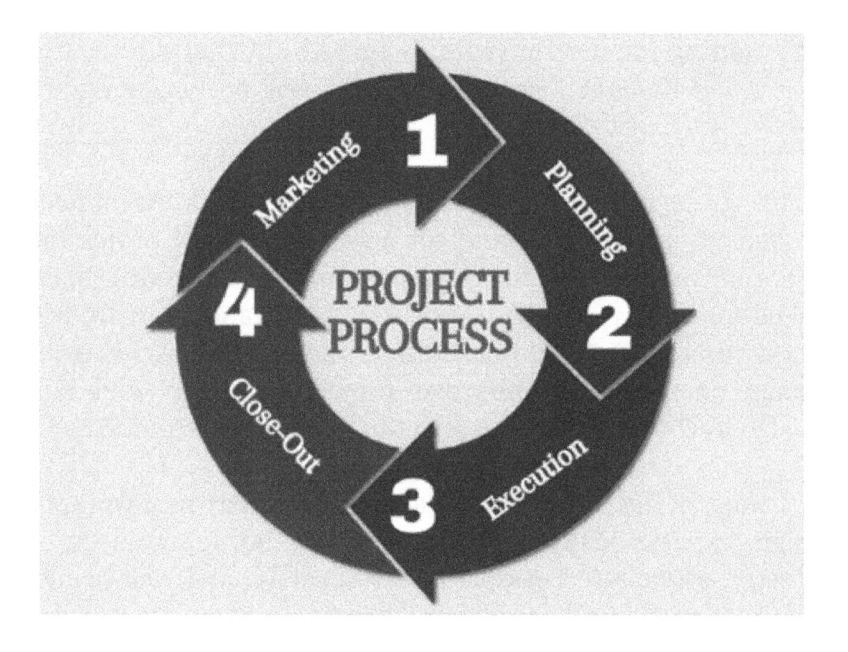

(Colorful Cycle Diagram Graph Template by Rizelle Anne Galvez on Canva)

In almost every industry, marketing efforts are considered overhead expenses. I cannot charge someone for services before I have the project! During the marketing process, I identify prospects, write proposals to potential clients for phases two through four, and plan how the company will complete the work if awarded the job. I always price the total proposal to cover marketing time with the client's profits (like I do other business expenses), but it is never a phase I get paid for.

Once a client agrees to the marketing proposal, the actual billable client work begins in phase two with planning. In developing the fee to charge the client, a plan is created for allocating employee time so the project is profitable, setting limits for staff hours per phase. Many of us (especially those of us in the more creative industries) tend to spend a lot of time upfront in the project planning phase, often more than allocated in the project profitability budget, leaving less of a fee than planned for execution and hardly any for close-out. Sometimes, the project scope increases, and the original fees no longer cover the work if new fees are not negotiated.

Unfortunately, I have seen more than one company abandon a project midway through phase four (i.e., close-out) because there was no fee remaining, so they could move on to the next profitable project. They would resent the time wasted on work that no longer benefits the bottom line. How do you think those projects turned out in the end? Do you think the clients hired them again for the next project and referred them to others? Or did they blame them for any final problems toward the wrap-up? Every entrepreneur learns that referrals and repeat business are the best marketing opportunities.

Keys to Flipping the Script

This is an example of where you can flip the script. Through my experiences with project work, I recognized a huge opportunity to set my services apart from others through a change in my mindset and internal fee management. Like others, my marketing is unpaid, and my project work begins in phase two. But if I wind up being short on fees in phase four, close-out, rather than leaving the work unfinished and risking the client not being satisfied, I will flow right into the marketing phase on my side. This is such a positive approach and turns any feelings of resentment into excitement. Finishing a project strong will lead to more repeat work and stronger referrals and is a much better use of time than cold marketing. This is a more effective way to market, as you demonstrate your value to your client and all other companies involved in the project. Remember: referrals can come from anyone!

How has this approach worked for me over the years? This past year alone, more than half of my project work is for repeat clientele, and I have a steady stream of referral work. I spend little to no time cold marketing or chasing new clients. This specific example of my personal aha moment might not work exactly the same way for you, but I have learned tips that apply to any business situation:

How can you flip the script in your work?

1. **Study the market.** Do you see a service gap that you could fill? Find what matters most to clients and prioritize that in your services. Remember, you might not need to offer the best product or be the cheapest option; exceptional service could be your clients' most important purchasing consideration.
2. **Highlight your strengths.** What do you do well? What makes you stand out from others in the industry, and how can you bring more of that to your clients?
3. **Don't just react—adapt!** As you work hard and reach your goals, you may realize they were not everything you dreamed they would be. You may be ready to change direction or realize that you have already set higher goals altogether. This is totally normal. Entrepreneurs need to adapt to current circumstances.
4. **Ask questions.** Challenge the norm. Examine the project's delivery and overall process and consider whether it has to be done this way or if there is something you can do to improve it.

5. **Be flexible.** Life is full of twists and turns. You might be going for the same outcome as your competition, but maybe you can do it differently. Think about all the different ways to tie our shoes—which is best? The one that works for you!

The more you follow your intuition, adapt to the situation, and be yourself, the more successful you will be, no matter your industry. I encourage you to flip the script on a business process and make it work better for you!

About Virginia

Virginia Weida has long been a woman who has positively influenced the commercial real estate industry and has never been satisfied with the status quo. She is the CEO and founder of Virginia Weida Designs, LCC, which was created in 2006, and has been thriving ever since. With over thirty-two years of experience, Virginia specializes in workplace strategy & design projects in Pittsburgh and the region with a strong track record of successfully completing deals with consistent results and a proven reputation in her market.

Virginia is an independent consultant and unicorn in her marketplace. She is an entrepreneurial, creative problem-solver passionate about all things CRE. Virginia credits her education at Cornell University for giving her a solid cornerstone to carve out a unique career path. Trained and certified as an interior designer, she became a certified facility manager (CFM), as well as a LEED and WELL certified professional to provide a trifecta of services within the office tenant marketplace. She has experience in professional, financial, legal, higher education, library, healthcare, hospitality, industrial, civic, and tech sectors. Virginia is an expert, offering a range of capabilities that maximize returns for owners and minimize headaches for tenants.

In addition to being a trailblazer in her professional career, Virginia is a respected leader and advocate in the CRE industry and local community and worked as an adjunct design professor for fifteen years. She has maintained her lifelong commitment to making a social impact by volunteering with national, regional, and local organizations, supporting her industry and local communities and small businesses, as well as uplifting women. Beyond many years of board service across her career, Virginia has held the president or chair role in national and local organizations four times in the last five years, receiving several awards for her contributions. She fervently believes that design impacts people, places, and the planet, and demonstrates high ethical standards, service, and excellence in every endeavor.

Virginia Weida

Connect with her on LinkedIn or Instagram, or through www.virginiaweidadesigns.com.

Never a Failure. Always a Lesson.

Jackie Williams

A temporary tattoo is scrolled across the inside of my left arm. It bears a reminder to me.

"Never a failure. Always a lesson."

That message would never have donned my arm in the early days of my career. However, it is because I accept that message that I am confident in penning this chapter today.

To paint the picture of who I was when I started this journey, imagine an over-caffeinated, calorie-counting, impeccably dressed twenty-one-year-old who had just graduated a semester early from Clarion University of Pennsylvania with a dual major in accounting and finance and a minor in economics.

The picture of someone who feared anything that resembled failure.

My husband enjoys recounting the days of me calling him in tears and a panic after taking college exams that resulted in a final college GPA of 3.99. My only B was a physical fitness exam in my one-credit "Beginning Tennis" course, which I only took to meet my physical education credit requirements.

The pressure I put on myself allowed me to graduate a semester early in December 2004 and move full steam ahead into the busy season at my dream job at the time, "Audit Associate" at a "big four" accounting firm in downtown Pittsburgh, Pa.

For those of us raised in the less populated region of northwest Pennsylvania, like Erie, where I grew up, Pittsburgh was *the* big city. I attended parochial schools from kindergarten to twelfth grade. My upbringing and relationship with God drew me to seek His direction in my life; to prayerfully explore and answer the call to my purpose in the world.

So, when the accounting fraud scandal at Enron erupted during my first semester of college around October 2001, I firmly believed it was a sign that God was calling me to a purpose as an ethical auditor of financial statements. At that moment, I decided that I should stop being an "undecided" major between psychology and accounting. I now had confidence that accounting was just not a greedy and certain career path, but that God was calling me to help people through accounting.

With an upbringing in a faith that strongly emphasized a need for regular confession and a somewhat less than compassionate view of failure in the classroom, I entered into a profession that prided itself in accuracy. It is with that perspective that I convey my understanding of success at the time: a steady upward climb like a staircase; a graph with an arrow pointing up and to the right, not a path of stepping stones that weave and wind to eventually get you to your destination.

I certainly didn't see failings as lessons or as stepping stones toward success. I was fiercely pursuing a career that was created to find others' failures and report them to the public!

So with that in mind, I entered a big four accounting firm's auditing department. And, boy, did I take my job seriously!

Perhaps too seriously.

I remember proudly finding my first "misstatement" of numbers during my test work in the spring of 2005. Based on my calculations, it was miscalculated to the tune of tens of thousands. I quickly made my way to my manager's office. He patiently listened to me and then gently reminded me of the very significant materiality threshold that our biggest client, who I was working on at the time, had and that, to my dismay, this misstatement wouldn't even make the list to be aggregated with other misstatements to determine if there was material misstatement.

He encouraged me to stay the course and explained that he hoped I would be the one to find a material misstatement for that client one day.

This was a valuable lesson. I didn't view my work as a failure but considered that maybe successful companies don't have failures—at least not material ones. This confirmed my definition of success being an arrow pointing up and to the right.

I was passionate about my work. I was determined to keep going up the trajectory outlined in big four public accounting. I wasn't going to progress in any manner but along a straight arrow, pointing up and to the right. I exceeded expectations on my performance reviews. I was promoted early to the coveted senior associate and manager positions. I did everything necessary to maintain the highest levels in this role, all the while maintaining a serious and fun relationship with my now husband, Adam, who was in law school at the University of Pittsburgh at the time. We married in August 2007 after five and a half years of dating.

All was going according to plan. We were living our best yuppie lives—arrows pointing up and to the right—regardless of how sleep-deprived we were.

That is, until the spring of 2009.

In May 2009, right after completing our first significant running achievement together—crossing the finish line of the half marathon course of the re-instated Pittsburgh Marathon—Adam and I learned that we were expecting our first child.

We were excited, and terrified. This was not exactly the timing we anticipated.

I remember standing in the shower the morning I took the pregnancy test, stunned. How would this impact my arrow and our joint arrow?

Nonetheless, excitement overwhelmed the fear, and we quickly headed to Half Price Books to get all the parenting and baby name books we could find.

A short two weeks later on June 5, 2009, at just over nine weeks pregnant, no heartbeat was detected on our first sonogram. We were told to anticipate miscarrying that weekend. On June 7th, I lost the baby.

It was at that moment that I was given my first opportunity to really learn how failure can be viewed as a lesson and that, with "failure," a very important quality for success, resilience is built. Without this lesson, I would have never had the success I have achieved and continue to achieve in life *and* business.

I took a week off and grieved. For a long time, I was angry and resentful of others who had the ideal first pregnancy experience. Over the next four months, I went into work pursuing a return to my "up and to the right" arrow as an audit manager, but that arrow just wasn't as fulfilling as it seemed before I thought I was going to be a mother. Actually, my purpose seemed empty when comparing it to the impact I could have had as a mother. In this space, failure seemed inevitable. Pushing back self-loathing and blame for the loss, I went through the motions but started looking for new job positions that would allow me to live my purpose, and allow me to take better care of myself instead of the high-pressure and stressful environment I was currently in.

By October of that year, I found exactly what I was looking for in an accounting policy position at a big bank. I would be able to work in my purpose to ensure accurate accounting for the investor public, but within much more manageable hours and in a lower-stress environment. During the first year of my employment, I was able to be involved in implementing the acquisition accounting for the acquisition of another large bank, and also successfully started growing our son, Royce, in my womb.

The arrow was back to pointing up and to the right, but perhaps at a less significant incline.

Within the first trimester that we were pregnant with Royce, Adam had the opportunity to pursue a clerkship with a judge in our hometown. This was the logical next step for the eventual establishment of his own law firm, which made more sense to start in Erie where we knew more people.

I was torn and afraid. I found a job that I loved and now I was pregnant. How would that work knowing that I would be moving into a new job in Erie?

This was not the timing I had been hoping for. Still, I worked on preparing my resume. Interestingly enough, that timing lined up with the bank pioneering flexible work arrangements that included telecommuting.

Not having much to lose given the decision to move anyway, I asked for what I wanted. I requested pioneering remote work, and my request was accepted! I worked for the bank for nearly ten years, with nine and a half of those years in a remote work arrangement! During that time, Royce joined our family, I grew my career at the bank as a reduced workweek professional and did the bookkeeping for Adam's law firm.

As time passed, we lost two more pregnancies, one single pregnancy and a twin pregnancy.

After I lost our third pregnancy, I shared the loss with my manager who had called me into her office to eagerly offer me a spot on the team that would be working to implement a new accounting standard that would significantly impact the banking industry.

I was honored to be considered and recognized as a key contributor to the team but expressed concern regarding whether an eventual successful pregnancy would be seen as a failure in this role. She encouraged me to pursue both.

With her support, I had another perspective on success. I joined a peer mentoring group at this time too. In that safe space, I learned that I was not alone in a need to persist and overcome to achieve success.

Through this newfound perspective, I further began building my resiliency muscle and probed doctors for answers, making each "failure" a lesson. Despite these failures, I chose to persist, eagerly taking on more challenging work by working on the adoption of the Current Expected Credit Losses standard at the bank *and* fiercely pursuing tests for answers with my doctors. Though I didn't know it at the time, I was attacking this situation as though failure was not inevitable or present. Rather, I was now moving as though success was inevitable—if I kept moving.

As a result of discovering and getting treated for my autoimmune thyroid disease, on June 13, 2017, I gave birth to our daughter Penelope. After Penelope joined us, I took on an even more challenging role at the bank. However, on March 19, 2019, I chose to leave that role to assist Adam in growing the law firm as he too was growing in persistence through setbacks and taking on professional and personal coaching, with much success. I believed that, if we worked together, we could build something great *and* spend more time with each other and our children.

Exactly one year after I left the bank, COVID shut down all non-essential businesses. This meant courthouses were closed too, which significantly limited the growth of the firm. At that time, some might say my decision to leave my secure position at the bank and put all of our eggs in one basket in the law firm was a failure.

We certainly did not.

As a matter of fact, it certainly helped that I knew *a lot* about how to successfully mentor a team to work remotely! We were able to see COVID not as a setback but as an opportunity.

Adam's example and drive to research and persist in protecting our employees' jobs, our livelihood, and the sanity of our small business owner clients and friends allowed us to work together to innovate and build services to help small business owners.

Adam took consults and provided webinars to small business owner clients to help them understand the COVID relief programs available to them. Together, we innovated product offerings that secured our clients over $5 million in forgiven

Payroll Protection Program loan funds and almost $75 million in Employee Retention Credit funds through thorough eligibility analysis and calculations.

Fast forward to today...we are building our new tax strategy firm, Pennywise Tax Strategies, to continue helping small business owners by helping them master their numbers, minimize their tax burden, and maximize their personal and business potential.

Throughout this entire journey, there have been setbacks, some of which cost us more than others. We call those costs "tuition," because it is what we are paying for the lesson. We implement the lessons and persist.

Coco Chanel is quoted as saying, "Success is often achieved by those who don't know that failure is inevitable."[2] As an avid fan and student of Chanel's, I have read that quote repeatedly trying to understand what exactly she meant by it. It took me quite a while to fully digest it: Do successful people act naive to failure? Do they not admit failings?

But now I understand that she meant that people who are considered successful don't accept failure, they embrace the lesson. They learn, pivot, and have faith to keep pursuing their goals and purpose.

The step to success I wish to share with you is to classify what others may see as "failures" as lessons. Don't let setbacks stop you. If you are someone who has had the experience of an arrow pointing up and to the right for the majority of your path and are experiencing a setback, your action at this time is crucial.

Choose not to accept failure as inevitable. Accept this setback as a lesson, as a stone crafting a bend in the winding stepping stone path of success forward.

---

[2] https://www.goodreads.com/quotes/52014-success-is-most-often-achieved-by-those-who-don-t-know

Steps to Success

There is not one defined path to success, and it is very likely not a straight line. In fact, your path will continue to evolve, and your persistence muscle will need to continue to be exercised.

You do have the power to succeed though, no matter where you are on that path. You decide whether a situation is a failure or a lesson.

Today, will you decide to approach a setback as an inevitable failure or as a lesson, as steps on the path to success?

About Jackie

Photo by Jessica Hunter (Jessica Hunter Photography - www.jessicahunterphotos.com)

Jackie Williams

Jacqueline Williams is a certified public accountant and a certified tax planner with a background in big four auditing and accounting policy at a Fortune 500 firm. During the pandemic, she was overjoyed to build systems to help small businesses obtain and keep funds available through the Payroll Protection Program and Employee Retention Tax Credit with Rust Belt Business Law.

As an accountant for around twenty years and married into an entrepreneurial family for over fifteen years, Jackie chose to meet small business owners where they are on their journey of understanding their numbers, building Pennywise Tax Strategies with her husband to help small businesses achieve financial success by keeping more of their hard-earned profits. Pennywise Tax Strategies helps small business owners proactively strategize saving money on their taxes and document their tax positions consistent with the tax code.

When she is not geeking out about saving tax dollars, Jackie serves on the finance committee of Emma's Footprints and enjoys running and Barre workouts, putting together a great outfit, singing karaoke, and driving her convertible (with a six-speed). She is a self-proclaimed self-development junkie and enjoys traveling and spending time with her husband, Adam; children, Royce and Penny; and dogs, Camber and Trixie.

You can follow her on Instagram: @faithfashionfinances. For more information on Pennywise Tax Strategies, you can visit our website at www.pennywise.tax, follow Pennywise Tax Strategies on Facebook, or follow us on Instagram @pennywise.tax.

Rig to Renewal: Turning Burnout into a Wellness Mission

Megan Wollerton

My alarm clock went off, and I couldn't reach the snooze button fast enough. I had taken three non-emergency calls throughout the night. I was exhausted, but I pulled myself out of bed, dressed, made a cup of coffee, and headed out for another day at the office as a service manager in the oil and gas industry. Our company provided housing, trucking, and equipment for the rig hands and drill site. I was told early in my career, "Those drill rigs run twenty-four hours a day, seven days a week," so I should expect to be on call twenty-four/seven.

This, of course, was an impossible task. It was easy for the drill site manager to tell me that—he only worked two weeks onsite and then got two weeks off. As for me, I worked sixty to one hundred hours a week, was on call twenty-four hours a day, and hardly got to take a vacation. Saying that I was burned out would be an understatement. On top of the demands of the job, it was a male-dominated field, and discrimination was rampant. I felt like I constantly had to prove myself and put in the extra effort to stay ahead of the male supervisors who were eager to take my job.

Then one day it happened. My boss, whom I never saw eye-to-eye with, finally found a reason to let me go. I was distraught. Thoughts of how I would pay my bills and where I would go with the skills I had learned flooded my mind. I had given everything to that organization, helped it grow, developed its processes, and my team was like my family. The first few weeks of unemployment went by in a blur. I was so lost I had no idea what to do with myself.

It was then I realized I had given everything to that company and lost so much along the way. I felt like a stranger to my husband. I had lost contact with friends and family with whom I was once so close. Worst of all, I had lost myself. Who was I? What did I enjoy? What made me unique? Financially stable thanks to my severance pay and my husband's steady employment, I decided to use this time to find myself again. Because of a one-year non-compete agreement, I couldn't find a job in my field anyway. That's when I started reaching out to friends and family again. I spent more time in the gym, got into competitive boxing, and fell in love with fitness.

About nine months later, I was transformed. I was at a healthy weight, and my Crohn's disease was finally under control now that the stress and anxiety of my job had been lifted. My husband and I reconnected, and our marriage started to flourish again. This is when my coach asked me, "How will you maintain your new healthy lifestyle when you return to work in the oil and gas field?" The dread of returning to the grind made me physically ill when he asked me that question. I felt like I was punched in the gut. My blood pressure spiked, and I could feel every muscle in my body tense. It was at that moment I realized I didn't belong there. That question sparked the aha moment in my life.

My response to my coach was simple: "I won't. Because I am not going back to the oil and gas industry." I worked with my coach and a friend who was a personal trainer to get guidance on how to become a fitness professional. In no time, I signed up with the American Council on Exercise to become a certified personal trainer. I used my remaining time on unemployment to hit the books and take my test. Before long, I was certified and landed my first job at a local upscale fitness club. I loved it. I was excited to start my journey and found a real specialty in teaching boxing classes. Within six months, I was booked to capacity with personal training clients and fitness classes, and I'd developed a following.

Growing my personal training business was exciting. Over the next few years, I pursued health and nutrition coaching certifications. I worked with clients inside the gym and took personal coaching clients outside the club. I was growing my own small business and experiencing a lot of success. It was exhilarating, and I felt like I was genuinely making a difference. My clients experienced transformations: losing weight, building strength, and developing confidence. My clients expected me to deliver results, and I met their expectations.

Word of mouth spread, and I accepted more and more clients. One day, the club announced its annual New Year's resolution competition for weight loss. I participated as a team leader and was shocked when I did my initial weigh-in. Where did the extra pounds come from? That is when I realized I had fallen into the same trap. My first client appointment was at 4:45 a.m., and my last was at 8:30 p.m. I was working all day, with only a few breaks in the afternoon. I left no time for my own workouts, and I wasn't eating properly between appointments. My business was booming, but I was burning out again. My husband would come to workout at the club just on the off chance we could catch a quick dinner together between clients. I was so exhausted on the weekends that my social life started to dwindle again. I was working on yet another certification when my husband came to me and asked, "What is it for? Who is this helping?"

I thought about what he meant and quickly understood that while I was helping others and making positive changes, it wasn't the demographic I wanted to work with. I hired a business coach who specialized in working with fitness professionals. I signed up for group coaching, and knowing I was not alone was nice. I made new friends with other fitness professionals who had the same struggles. We all recognized that there are only so many hours in a day, and we needed to be more selective about how we spent that time. My coach helped me determine what parts of my job I enjoyed, who I wanted to help, what my specialty was, and what I wanted for my life. With coaching, I learned that I cannot be everything to everyone. I worked with a wide range of clients from ages five to eighty-five. Some wanted weight loss, others wanted to manage disease, and others wanted to build strength. I was stretching myself too thin and had lost focus on why I started a fitness career in the first place.

My coach made me look at my business from a new perspective. Instead of people-pleasing and trying to help everyone, we discussed what I enjoyed, how many hours a week would be ideal for me and my now-growing family, how much money I wanted to make, and other plans I had for my life. We considered which demographic I had a heart for. Who were the clients I enjoyed helping the most? It was through this process that I crafted my mission. I wanted to help people like me—people in corporate America—putting their health and well-being on the back burner for a chance to climb the corporate ladder.

I knew that when I was in the thick of it, I wasn't looking for a coach, I was just trying to keep my head above water. My coach and I discussed how I could reach those people and make a real impact on their lives. I developed a plan to launch Life Force Wellness, a corporate wellness consulting company. If I could teach leaders in organizations the importance of watching out for their employees' well-being, I could save others from experiencing the same struggles I went through.

My goal was clear: transform corporate cultures so employees can thrive, not just financially but physically and psychologically as well. By collaborating with leaders and their employees, I can end burnout, eliminate the "Sunday Scaries," and help others enjoy their work as much as I do while protecting their well-being. I then pursued certifications in positive psychology and stress management to address the issues employees face head-on. I enjoy teaching company leaders the importance of caring for their employees and creating healthy, positive work cultures. I also enjoy teaching employees the importance of developing healthy habits, making time for self-care, and setting boundaries.

Most importantly, I ensure that I practice what I preach. It is so easy for us to drive ourselves to burnout, so I developed a free life-balance assessment. If you feel burned out, you can use this tool to help you see which area you might be neglecting so you can refocus and find the balance you need. (https://lifeforcewellness.com/balance). Remember, no matter how noble the cause is, you must still care for yourself to better care for others.

About Megan

Megan Wollerton

B.S. Business Administration/Marketing, Minor in Psychology - Edinboro University
Certified Personal Trainer, Certified Health Coach, Certified Nutrition Coach, Certified Corporate Wellness Specialist, Certified Positive Psychology Practitioner and Certified Stress Management, Sleep and Recovery Coach.

Megan Wollerton, owner of Life Force Wellness LLC, is a certified personal trainer, health coach, nutrition coach, corporate wellness specialist, and positive psychology practitioner. She is also a stress management, sleep, and recovery coach. With a B.S. in business administration/marketing and a minor in psychology, Megan has a passion for creating engaging corporate wellness programs that work for both employees and employers.

After experiencing burnout working long, stressful hours in the tumultuous oil and gas field, Megan decided to break out on her own and focus on health and wellness. She recognized the importance of work-life balance and created a program that would benefit herself and her employees. Since then, Megan has been helping clients achieve happier and healthier lifestyles through her expertise in exercise, nutrition, mental resiliency, behavior change, and well-being. Megan brings her passion for wellness into the corporate environment by collaborating with leaders to transform company cultures, emphasizing employee health and wellbeing. Her mission is to create psychologically safe and less toxic working environments where employees can thrive.

At Life Force Wellness, Megan focuses on seven distinct areas of well-being. With her dedication to helping others and extensive knowledge of wellness, she is committed to providing effective solutions that lead to happier and more productive employees for companies.

About the Alzheimer's Association

The authors in this book hope their stories encourage you to find your aha moments and use those to build your steps to success. These stories illustrate that sometimes the unknown is scary, but to have that success professionally or personally, you must keep moving forward.

The curator of these wonderful author chapters, Denise Ann Galloni, chose the Alzheimer's Association as the nonprofit that will benefit from the online sales of this book through Aurora Corialis Publishing. A portion of these sales will go directly to the Alzheimer's Association in an effort to help eradicate memory loss diseases such as Alzheimer's and dementia. This is a special cause near and dear to Denise Ann's heart as she lost her mother, Sylvia Goodfellow to one of these devastating diseases, and several other authors in this book have experienced this heartbreak in their own families.

The Alzheimer's Association is a national nonprofit that leads the way to end Alzheimer's and other forms of dementia through education about early detection, support, and accelerating global research. To learn more about this organization and to find local chapters in your area, visit www.alz.org.

Steps to Success

Sylvia and Robert Goodfellow on their wedding day

About the Alzheimer's Association

Sylvia Goodfellow, Denise Ann's mom, and Denise Ann